TO REHUMANIZE

Poetry by Andrei Novac

Lyrico Press

www.lyricopress.com

To Rehumanize, Poetry by Andrei Novac

Published by Lyrico Press

www.lyricopress.com

contact@lyricopress.com

Cover by Jonathan Levley

ISBN-13: 978-1707889686

Dedication

This book is dedicated to creative minds who are working quietly and tirelessly to alleviate suffering and make this a better world.

Acknowledgments

To Bonita, my life companion and love, who has encouraged me never to give up writing and has inspired my latest endeavors.

With gratitude to my loved ones at home: Bonita, Irene, Rachel, Allegra and Nono.

To Alexandra and Puck, my loving Romanian family in Europe.

Special thanks to Irene Novac, my editor.

Thanks to Jonathan and Deborah, who have made this project possible.

ix

Table of Contents

Foreword

To Rehumanize is a work in progress arising out of a struggle. It is the struggle with the question: "What keeps us humane when facing sustained adversity?"

With our technological means to create illusions of physical proximity, at a deeper level, isolation has been an ever-growing plight of contemporary human times. It is possible today to exchange volumes of words with someone outside our physical space without ever seeing any human face, feeling their emotions, their chemistry, or understanding their motives.

Henry Bergson examined the notion of habit, a way of acting, reacting and seemingly assimilating the environment, without particular awareness and planning.[1] In this sense, this volume approaches the remedy of contemporary dehumanization, precisely from the point of view of changing our habits. In doing so, we are rethinking awareness and space, two different dimensions of possible altruism in human society.

As in ancient times, I am proposing that words can exorcise past transgressions and the neglect of humans towards other humans as well as the loss of value of social existence. As with words created by the masters of antiquity, today poetry remains a relatively untapped source of healing from the violating effect of everyday depersonalized encounters.

As in any healing process, this volume proposes a gradation through stages. To be able to rehumanize our spirit, it is necessary to first proceed through the darkest moments of existence. Therefore, the first chapter "Dystopia" proposes that our dimming lights could, in fact, further darken. Yet, visiting dystopia may actually be a welcoming journey, a necessary loss of innocence before the veil of blessed reason is again bestowed upon us.

Similar to history, philosophy and hermeneutics, which interpret reality and thoughts,[2] poetry as a method may shape cultural values that further expand into the human core. The tone of poetry may promote enduring novel holistic and humanistic forms of communication. I would submit that selective words are still to be rediscovered to expand universal, enlightened values. Such words and their values would serve as an antidote to obfuscation that we experience in times of cold emotional isolation. Currently, the world seems to show a precipitated move towards artificial segregation into many different groups in a process that Erik Erickson named decades ago as "pseudospeciation."[3] Influenced by fear, we have created new human subgroups, the Others, that have no reasons to exist except for protecting us from our own demons.

Rehumanizing, the reverse process of dehumanization, is hard. It starts in a raw form each day: honor a peer every day without a particular motive, and you will be honored back in multiples.

I decided to collect these poems written in 2018 and 2019, ahead of a planned volume on Trauma and the Repair of Wounds. For the poet, the cure may have to be delivered before disease is exposed. *To Rehumanize* tries to capture a variety of moments, unplanned states and spontaneous responses that reflect our need to connect on a human level. Like spontaneous creativity, these moments may be daily occurrences. Poetry may help to recognize such innocuous moments as gateways into an expanded human universe.

The first section, *Dystopia*, was inspired by listening to world news.

Those who study memory and consciousness tell us that forgetting is as important as remembering. And where does a world go to, when all personal and world history is stored, to be remembered forever? The opening poem, "Forgetting," is a direct irony addressed to Zeus and his cohort in Heaven. It is also an irreverent examination of deity into allowing the world to sink into this deep hole. Does Zeus know about starving children and failed plans to transform cannonballs into "molds of golden ages?" Is God aging and has not kept up with human deeds? And yes, "Have humans forgotten to forget?" In the next poem "Why You Don't See," the refrain "...but it's no longer me, and you cannot see" is a plea for caution about no longer hearing each other. And immediately following, old friends no longer spend nights together, talking, debating. Those friendships, which promote openness and acceptance, are touches of God. Themes of dignity lost, the Golden Calf, the idols that abound today, compromise our ability to dream and become whole again. "Nighttime Visitation" was inspired by a reported double murder, an act that made the clouds watch and cry.

Resistance, the second section, portrays the internal workings of human resiliency and the wish to reestablish social relations of decency. With 13 poems, it is this volume's most extensive chapter. "Forgetting Not" is a story of a secret loving encounter between survivors of a global catastrophe. Immediately following, "Henid" refers to seeds of mental constructs that may become turning points in one's thinking. Henid is the simplest psychological fact or a "half thought," a concept described by the philosophers Otto Weininger and Sir Bernard Williams.[4] It occurs as a vestigial core and creative process of a becoming notion in our mind, a "cipher" to the opening of time.

There are other themes linked to enhancing cognition and consciousness: "San Pedro" opens doors; "Mirror Vision" offers alternative to the plight of both "carrying stones at day and navigating dark seas at night." They will, in time, allow you to "see" or gain new perspectives. There is reemergence of communication in "Knowing of Knowing" and "Penetrating Journey" ("pouring on a world of souls"). "The Southern Ocean Floor" contains krill, mini-creatures that maintain life and memory of earth, similar to our bodies that maintain perceptive memories of life.

The third chapter, *The Other Side of the World* brings back the theme of the journey. These are poems written away from home, often in remote places where the local scenery and culture served as a source of insights and inspiration. These poems shall serve as encouragement for the reader to undertake personal journeys of discoveries and growth. Here, the old Flemish masters inspire a collective voice to say "No" to the next war. Each trip in life is a potential emotional and spiritual experience meant to expand one's vision and horizon when our mind becomes myopic and short-circuited.

Finally, *Rehumanize* is meant to be the final purpose of this collection. It offers a transition to the future. There are playful times of snowflakes and city sounds and unfinished thoughts and cricket songs. Among other examples, the ubiquitous "Neutrino" is pure energy to inspire us, to revive our world. Meditating on the "Neutrino," the smallest existing element, reminds us of the labor of scientists that have been tracing time and history in the layers of permanent snows of the Antarctic. Similarly, the structure of human sound and our words can take us back to the pre-archeological times of our consciousness. Here love and play and soul together create a locus of endurance.[5]

A.N.
Newport Beach, California
November 2019

References

1. Bergson, H. (1896/1991). Matter and memory, trans. N.M. Paul and W.S. Palmer. New York: Zone.

2. Eliade, M. (1969). *The quest: History and meaning in religion.* University of Chicago.

3. Erikson, E. (June 1985). Pseudospeciation in the nuclear age. *Political Psychology,* Vol. 6, No. 2, Special Issue: A Notebook on the psychology of the US–Soviet relationship, pp. 213–217.

4. Weininger, O. (2005). Trans. Ladislaus Lob. Daniel Steuer introduction: Sex and character: An investigation of fundamental principles. Indiana University Press (1903).

5. The poem was inspired by Amy Wallen's book *When we were ghouls: A memoire of ghost stories.* University of Nebraska Press (2018).

To Rehumanize

Poetry by Andrei Novac

I

Dystopia

Forgetting

Zeus, when on the mount, we called on you, you ordered:
"Stop mankind's torrential stilted thoughts, offensive gestures and murderous intentions."

Come on, you can change even the weather, Zeus!
Have you forgotten how the world's hurricanes have wiped out our depth?
Have you ever seen your children starve?
Did you see the crowds begging for food?

Oh Zeus, you once boasted to own hail and fire,
To let cannon copper melt into new molds of golden ages.
Still trying to transform the winds of war into the breeze of universal friendship?
Now, as laughable a promise as they seemed once to be the only accepted truth.

Oh Zeus, have you met lately with counsel, Elohim, Wotan, or Holy Ghost?
What do they think?
Or are they plagued like you, by similarly aging mind and slowing bowel?
Zeus, do you remember when logic and reason were reigning the earth?

Have humans forgotten to forget?
For semi-erasure of stories to be given a proper burial.
Instead, long, unforgiving memories,
No longer allow deliverance from darkened history referral.

Why You Don't See
(To a world of madness)

Walls have risen between us all,
You watch the screen, you see my face,
You seem to recognize a trace
But it's no longer me,
And you cannot see.

You see and hear the words
Caresses of some sorts,
A music of my voice,
With no real choice
But it's no longer me,
And you cannot see.

I can no longer hear a real-world reason,
Strange handlers of facts are beyond choices,
To reset faces, words and voices
But it's no longer me,
And you cannot see.

Virtual impostors now grooming.
Emotionally corrupt and looming,
A world of hearts sold out for the season
With money from the top for clear treason,
Humanely, morally deemed mad
Historically, as future, dead.

To My Friend

Once, not too long ago
We were friends talking and chatting through
the night.
In nightly celebration, features of our fallen aura, the
lost walls of socially-protected falsehoods.

Those walls, when still strong
Kept tears from rolling and fears from spreading.
Now it is as we embraced each other more,
That life is made of many curtain calls.

Curtains have risen and fallen many times for us.
Curtains raised, do not always make a showing for a
good show.
When curtains fall and silence comes on, there is no
need for goodbyes and brokenhearted talk.

Did mom not want to lose me as a baby?
Was I supposed to grow up?
A gentle look at history, how love engulfs
the human soul.
The bliss, the touch of God
The growth into nurturance.
Love given growth, riches of life,
remembers redemption.

Missing Puzzle

Is memory an ethereal being?
A ghost that hovers over decent souls;
Plagued and unredeemable souls?
A sign from God that your work is incomplete?
Re-creations that you cannot return to their senders?

How many tortured hours to endure,
To pass the bar of granted peace of innocence?
A self, seeming released at last,
Into an abyss of deep indulgence...

Few hours in deep sleep?
Memory of love finally lost?
A missing body, now shivering alone?
Hours of longing, for wanted peaks of unity
previously hast.

Can your rebellion be released at last to make peace
with your urging spirit?

Swaying Hours

In a sheltering encasement
You travel the times,
You can travel the Heights.
Paying in hours it takes to first hear and see,
Dreaming of new seasons
For a world still to come and be.

The stories of summer
The words of four corners.
My legends never written
But shared by children in hunger.

Daily prayer in each one's own tongue.
Translate into joint power and song.

A song of the world we inherited here
A song of redemption from callous forgetting.
A song of no more making of the abandoned
No longer trailed by impositions on the mishandled.

Can we redeem dispelled dreams and cessations
And see, blink by blink, all new life constellations?

Return to a global love plasma of
Spirited freedom
And revive the love of human nature and seasons.

Your Far Away Corners

In a corner of a swaying spirit
Time is taken hostage by images of exotic journeys.
Touring the world from one end to another
I discover innocuous spaces that can propel you to
heaven.

A place with little room left for dignity;
Where sacred encounters are denied and
Viewing of noble souls are all forgotten.

Innocuous spaces open for you to exist.
Awakening your spirit on your own,
By rediscovering
Your perpetual ebb and flow of time.

Linking scenes from second to second
Like a strip of motion picture
From an old silent film
Now stitched together into a new garb,
Your imago of a new future.

Breaking up the Times

Who are we all beyond the fog of flowing time,
Hour after hour?
Are deep encounters doomed to perish
into obscure lamentations?
Waiting for an awakening to celebrate
the motionless sleeping beauty?

Alchemy, melting shapeless elements of
wrath and sorrow,
into a totemic block of soil,
Designated as the newly-found Golden Calf,
Wrapped duly into the emperor's new clothes.
Mocking the prophet's words,
Assigning a new machine as minted guardian spirit.

My dear, my future is too hard for me
to comprehend.
Yet some signs of thorough remorse of our world,
Allow me to see continuity of future resurrection.
Magic sweets, wrapped in cellophane,
Sounds of golden flutes.
All nurturing the souls of the new.
All waking.
If they can bring us back, to dream again,
Again.

Shattered Mold

A mold of my heart
Inside your inner mirror.
In myriad shades of diamond glitter.
Now at a total standstill. A sudden arrest of life.

My heart at a total standstill. Stunned.
Will it revive? Or dry and die?
Unknown, uncertain.

Now lost and rejected,
From moment to moment, feeling hour to hour.
Merciless state:
Deeply-knifed, your back turned.
Last word tried to utter but not heard:
Eternal love, it's yours!

Nighttime Visitations

Penetrating images shatter an equanimity
of wellbeing.
Three faces appear at night.
Three souls, defined now by an ephemeral
intersection of fate.
One, a mother who used to be visited
by high-minded dreams, now shattered forever.
Two, a father who used to play with fire and atoms.
Whose daily visiting friends were drawing
energy and power.
Three, another mother with tears and wisdom
in her ears, in her eyes,
giving nurture to many.
Tonight, a sacerdotal veil over a region with
offerings of dreamy clouds over ocean and land.
Now the clouds are watching and crying.
The Eternal too is here, learning of their lives and
unplanned humility.
Humility and dignity are fraternal twins of an
unrecognized father.
In an angry, fallen world, they shall banish evil
spirits into strangers' exiles.

II

Resistance

Forgetting Not

Mysterious hours, time suspended.
I am awakened by the bells of midnight towers.
No moon, no celestial blinking universe above,
Just darkness and an open path
For ancient forest creatures
Unknown to human sight of cast.

Who can forget?
It was a summer night
When smells of aging grass
And sounds of chords from late-night lovers
Still echoed into the early-hour darkness.

A side door opened, deadly night of passion
Walking into an embrace, primordial, unforgiving.
A thousand promises written in flesh and bone
And marked eternal unity played out in one embrace.

Memories still gather now.
From river shores calmly resounding,
From sound and scent of motion
Of bodies contorted to a human core.
From mild night winds and quiet laughs and lovers'
whispers.
Of love,
No might of hurricane has ever shorn.

Henid

Henids are trails left behind
Like overflowing waterways
that fertilize the barren land.
Henids, are seeds of mighty revelation
blessed by an almighty hand.

Half-full, half-delivered,
They are unintentionally unintelligible,
But have a shape of the generating Divine mold.

Henids visit your cluttered mind
To give you a seed of new hope
when life is unkind.
A cipher to a crossing of time
A secret code to your future to find.

Dreams on San Pedro

O Peter, Piotr, Petre, ultimate medicine.
Your wings are spreading into a new abyss.
The world I never met, was never allowed to explore.
Two men onto a journey.
A third man traveling along.

The dawn of life, a script of many
personal awakenings.
Did I encounter a new dimension
of moral preservation,
A face of fire and earth not given to man to explore?

A door I've searched the skies and seas for,
But never saw to emerge for me.
A long-traveled path to reach.
And then, to replay the story until infinity.
Infinity, where intersected worlds split off
Into an ultimate fused perpetual renewal.

Mirror Vision

I now have seen you in a mirror
The sweet flighty emerging youth
Returning to your eyes and face.
And needing nothing else.
From day to day, another world without regrets.
Just flights into the abyss of sudden love,
Free to explore, alone, still everyone along
Setting in motion the entire universe.

The other side,
A wish to strive between the walls
Of a permanent loving ground:
A space to play but never to be played,
A space of steady morning embrace.
When sun and love and morning sparks
All morph into words of a lasting bond.
Day in, day out.

Searching for Relief

Changes of rejuvenation ceased.
Crying, re-instituted.
Attempts to reconnect, now futile.
Are these relics?
Thoughts from the depth of an iceberg?
Carried by me like one of Sisyphus' stones?

A stone-carrier by day
A dark sea navigator by night.
Two highly "skilled" professions
Needing great talent and persuasion,
Just to be complete in their potential for destruction.

And yet, a persistence in me seeking your presence.
Your technicolor words and titles of images you
allowed me to see.
Your recognition of authenticity.
Your beauty and fine tastes and challenging
statements translated into pictures.
Your power to arouse feelings of sensuality.
Your gift to be, which makes me want to see you and
your being.
Speak up my dear muse! Don't turn into a shadow!
Come to me, tell me your story of the present!

Southern Ocean Floor

I never wanted to be seen,
Acknowledging lines of time upon my arrival.
The ocean floor, remote and unforgiving,
Remembers all but never tells.

It keeps decanted memories
For perpetuity to remember.
Acts and facts can now stand
When all are too eager to forget.

The floor, where great-grandmother Earth
found respite
A permanent refuge here, in the power of darkness.
Sitting in silence and never forgetting
Watching and waiting, for us to return to our senses.

Memory is a goddess of time, a sacred energy,
Perpetually feeding regeneration.
Hardly acknowledged for its essence but kept,
In molecules of soils and cells of life,
Like ancient Cassandra, harboring tales for the
future.

Knowing of Knowing

Reflecting on traces of love,
The awakening power of a smoldering fire.
Sheltered from view by fear of discovery.
Smoldering, an abyss away.
Do I really know my own depth?
Instances of life framing, remodeling.
An old script, handed down without questions asked.
Now discovered,
Promises received, or beliefs abandoned?

Penetrating Journey

The drill of life entering your space
Then, the first barrier of clouds encountered.
Sharpness becomes bluntness,
in touch with your clouds.
Your clouds of spirit, the gates of your heaven.
With layers of sound, myriad harmonies holding
each other
Like lovers locked in perpetuity by predestined
stories of their past.
Layers of harmonies, guarding your sacrament
of beauty.
The music of your sacred beauty, steadfast.

Hidden behind the vast land of your golden clouds,
Rising tall, the gates to souls.
Clouds of gold, sounds, deep layers of musical
harmonies, anticipated beauty.
Arrived at the ethereal gates of your souls,
I see pulsating powers.
From behind the ethereal gates I see energy of the
sun shining.
A golden waterfall of life and giving,
Pouring on a world of souls, of hungry beings.

Someone Talked to You

When someone talks to you
And it is real,
What do you hear?
Is it my voice or yours?

Shifting places, between thirsty souls
creates new spaces of germination.
Two cells, two thoughts, two molecules
Becoming fertile into one new spirit.

My name is New,
Born of two shining beings.
Cells by day, beams of light by night.

And so, my dear,
I am a changing fountain.
Seeming flesh when holding on to dance,
Still wanting love and tight embrace.
A hidden beam when watching in disguise
wanting no more than a front-row seat.

Asking Questions, Wise?

When love is under siege by its own lovers,
The siege remains unacknowledged, but felt.
And hours, days in lonely solitude
are permutations of old teenage heartbreaks.

Now dejected and small,
By forces beyond a hurricane's waves.
Long and past, the many hours
now seem mature and grown.

Aroused by uncontrollable thoughts
The immediacy of incessant questions asked
Frenzy, but in the making:
Wisdom or foolishness?

Inverted Stanzas

My words, inverted,
Never to reach your deepest meaning
Words, feeling reduced to fear of fear,
And solitary parting.

Without the launching of a couplet order,
Words of our world, remain unanswered questions.
Redemption attempted,
But sores already inflicted
Onto inner ghosts, glaciers and bedtime stories.

When Legends Speak

A new legend is rumored,
On sidewalks and behind windows
Animated faces, glowing cheeks, moist eyes.
But no one wants to meet my soul today.

The fruits have fallen, branches are barren
And no one is here to face with me.
Alone, they all have muted their compassion.
No immunity from feeling hanging night after night.

Trees in blossom.
The lilies, like whispers, spread in a pond.
Walking backwards through a starless night,
Meeting meteorites on their journey in full might.

Flowers return in the morning.

III

The Other Side of the World

Conversion Zone

Sailors of the far seas
Have known the waterways too well.
Passing the range of good fortune,
The seas maintain a circling border.
An edge, a barrier, a no man's land,
Where water suddenly feels melted ice
and ships keep a predestined course.

A miraculous force of nature,
A mighty delivery of transition
to the frozen continent.

Unlike nature, imagined human borders
Create firm statements.
Yet, like a word written in sand
over a transit territory,
Human borders are washed to slush by waves at sea.
They test our innocence when faced with shifting
hearts and times.

Auckland

Your restless arms stretched out
to many hungry vessels.
Incessant building and rebuilding lives
The bustling streets in summer heat,
The many faces of one people joining in at sunrise.

City, your many islands resting
on mighty earth of fire
Your many islands, kisses to your pulsing sea,
Give me an hour of your life's shape and beauty
An afternoon of lightning hours of new life.

In morning hours you move your cranes,
your mighty arms.
From shore, distant harmonies,
beginning chords of daily living.
Arriving for your morning chats and handshakes,
Young souls saving a planet
from reckless happenings.

The Day of Awakening

A summer evening in the Antarctic
When all souls awaken slowly.
Remembering a balmy afternoon,
A new space of gratitude
Bestowed by deep bonds of eternal love.
Built and rebuilt by karma,
Maintained by magic,
Awakened first by cabalistic genesis.

There was a day of awakening,
The day of sunrise.
Mountains of expectations were miraculously gone.
Acknowledgement finally emerged.

My love for you will never fade.
Your eyes glitter in alertness,
They have love's eternal power,
They feed a fire never to cease.

Aspen Future

Searching here for a future,
Germinating life as a mold
High mountain energy offerings
A spirit never to be old.

It was a night of full moon,
Eclipsing stars of life, they matter.
Life at the age of dreaming worlds
In all their beauty, old molds shatter.

New strings to free journeys
Are opening your eyes.

Alhambra Love

Open your eyes, my beauty
The music of your future shines.
Each string vibrates in love
And your voice yearns for one more measure of this
love song to repeat forever.

When charms of strings have entered
your permanent space,
Then, your heart has been enchanted forever.

Hospital in Flanders – Brugge

Ancient canal, the doors obstructed, closed.
The brick walls from a Flemish painting.
Faced by anyone wanting to come and see,
The real face of wars with hidden human faces.

A countdown over time,
St. John's, a running hospital for a million souls,
From Middle Ages to nineteen seventy-seven.
A Flemish color palette, a canal, the crying out of
wounded, in battles by the sea.
Cures of time, life given as a legacy to modern ages.

The sight of sites only in memory now,
Of blood and rotting, open wounds,
Obstructed by a palette of multicolored walls.

The world in twilight now,
With elixirs and potions sold with
Machiavellian taste,
Now still in use, to silence and to blind.

The art of Flanders, alive as ever,
As if old Masters, still toiling behind easels and
facing living ghosts.
Forever asking myriad questions, visible and heard,
but rarely remembered.
Keep asking. Keep asking.

You Inspire

You inspire an image, a story, a new thought,
A breath of love.
You inspire numbers,
The numbers of hours
The hours of waiting and longing.
You inspire spring,
When waiting and longing
Become numbers of flowers
And numbers of hours of blue sky
And music and dances and dreams
And eternal bliss.

Buenos Aires

Evening, summer.
The city is passing by like a torch of times.
A past cliché of tango cloud, spread overnight.
Here, tango is not a cliché
But sounds and perfumes of this evening,
Full of past regrets, now swollen in a mass
of patina gold.

They all bring awakening of one's evening senses.
Shadows of old hopes,
Hopes dressed up in shirts
that all tie up in black rhythms, face to face,
Awake through bitter fog of melancholic,
longing tongues.

The Other Side of Your World

When traveling to Akaroa
You can complain about the fog.
Beyond what I see are the contours of love.
Figurines, symbols of forgotten heroes
Parade music in the mist, for all to savor.

The fog is lifting
The New Zealand dawn, a brand-new chapter.
The dreams of the past strivings reappear.
The center of this earth, where flames of passion
ignite in hiding.

Revelations from Old Masters

Dark shadows to know the wisdom of a world
seemingly unbalanced.
Immersive for outsiders, but still alive.
A flame of life guiding a sense of joy.

The Flemish masters, sages of lessons, still here for
all the mortals,
Talked to the few, read by many, retold by some.
Watching dark shadows and hearing the questions to
the young:

When called again for the next war,
Will you once more say no, before?
Will you relinquish force's sores,
Become the old collective soul?
For all, once more.

Flanders, Belgium

IV

Rehumanize

New Islands Discovered

Oceans surround or are surrounded.
Descending is climbing down into new space.
Slowly, your eyes decipher contours.
Innocuous spaces become cells,
Demarcations of spiritual trials
packaged as corner islands,
unveiling the dwellings of morphed forms of life.

Next, corners of consciousness seem to exist.
Ubiquity is not ubiquitous.
Details of one small corner
Provide the beauty of isolated blooming,
Revealing shells and clothing of a detailed world.

Antarctic Neutrino

Antarctica, a name of shadows,
The stage of life when being is a form of energy.
A labyrinth of mindless disruptions,
Dwelling on details of a world without a soul,
It all set loose my wish to search for particles
of hope.

Neutrino, dimension that coexists but never reaches
independent reality.
No awareness, no acknowledgement of being.
A name given by science.
A zodiac without prediction of the future.

Pure energy of living in the present,
Neutrino, powerful, ubiquitous, invisible.
"N" lives in us, a changing shadow,
Generations regenerating ahead of us.

Judgment of Time

How far are trees from our fingertips?
Is our growth accounted for
By the sharpness of our tongue?
The fever of your forehead,
Packed in with lines of past discoveries?

Memories recover slowly.
The morning dew of numerous encounters,
The boundless joy of open inspirations,
Reawakened by the light of hope.
Now growing
into a clockwork beating pulse of love,
A perpetual seeking and unsettled heart.

Enthusiasm in Snowflakes

Hour by hour, mounts of heavy snow are now
engulfing my city.
Young and old cuddle under heavy blankets.
Cozy warmth, melting hearts into a melodic unison.
The dance of warmth felt by lovers from skin unto a
hungry soul.

In those hours life peaks,
Love returns in winter melancholy;
You lose count of time.
Seconds feel like incessant glitter
From restless souls like sparkling diamonds.

Tonight a deep layer of snow,
Parting present from future
The dance of snowflakes
Moving like wings engaged into a dance of life
Celebrating the random peaks
of our artistic freedom.

New York

In Dark Night

In dark night, the color of skin changes
at candlelight.
While the flame burns its way through the night,
Hearts whisper an unintelligible chat of eternal bliss.
The sculpture of two embracing bodies,
elongated by flames of longing,
Finding solace from the world in a long night of
moving shadows.
What is a night of love?
A gift offered incessantly, an elixir infused that
inebriates you into a new world.
A world where passion spreads into your being,
permanently.

How it Feels After

Glitter, deceptively gray sunset,
The light of a rainy spring afternoon
When sunset hours face the face of winter clouds
In darkened skies a golden pass, awake,
in sight.

Thought flashed.
Winking into space, an empty gesture.
Then comes a look into abyss, still nondescript.
Then, inner grasp takes shape,
still neutral and fleeting.
Then shimmering thought, amorphous and compact.

Awakened feelings bring color into
a mental painting,
Slowly erupting into chromatic hymns.
A peak of polytonal, orgiastic dances,
Celebrating a new order of expressive souls.

Dance, a ritual initiation,
Don't stop, you Gods of animals, excited.
You deep bearers of lots of untamed modes,
Open the door for lonely and lost faces
As sunshine looms in over-ecstatic growth.

Returning

Awake for your last stop of words.
I see your bright eyes opening into a pristine space.
Waking up the second time and finding a new life.
The sky of tomorrow, visible now
Through the fire of joyful rebirth.

Who is in your space?
How far deep is it to your heart?
Where are the passwords to your loving soul?
Sing me your songs.
Tell me your magic lines, the keys to your love.

Soundtracks of a City

Unfolded chunks of life, anonymously,
A stage-play in progression,
while it is being written.
Capturing freefall, chaos,
the hours when images collide.
An ancient anchor, still holding at bottom of a sea.

New lines, new actors, and new extras,
trying to make their strenuous case.
But seemingly, not fully told or listened to
Or comprehended.

A flowing symphony, exotic but exhausted,
Harmonies and words that just have lost their place.
Hardly comprehensible in style or meaning,
A constant humming in consciousness, a collective.

New York

Untold Storylines

Hieroglyphics in a carved soul.
With stripes of time still waiting to return.
Glowing, flowing, swaying,
Rewritten miles of DNA into one single thought.

Meeting in darkness and in bitter frost of time.
Joining those who are there to resonate as mine
Waking, staging, reviving, who you are at last.
Revolted faces of my soul, tall, visible a mast.

Meeting. Faces appear, devoid of any story,
any structure.
Like muted strains of movements.
Then blasting light in blinding mirrors
Living strips, reflections of your past re-awakened
on an easel.

Unfinished

Away, I miss you all again,
And, even more, when time is ticking.
A story replaying in my sound.
It scores muscular feels of living.

Who asks new questions?
Still growth from here but where?
Time can be your guardian,
Time can be your sore.

And then comes waiting, consenting again
A long night more thoughts of thoughts in sight,
Again, it shall be bright...

Cricket Song

The soothing breath of night, a wind of awe,
Your heart to recognize a code of whispers.
A state of recollection, in balmy summer quarters,
Reopening a world of yours ahead to know.

In silence a trance, revival of dreams as signals
of dawn,
A night of a thousand melodies, dissipating slowly.
Like a chatter of clouds blown away by air exhaled
by a rising sun.
The cricket song, muting away to sleep another day
away.

Play

Revival, reveal yourself to me.
My hungry soul, thousands of years old.
My eyes have seen centuries of sweet surrender
now frozen into a block of time.

Waiting. Sitting out each moment.
Time, a dripping stalactite,
Each drop, a painstaking remake,
Sensing inside the flowing nature of life.

Love and play and soul,
together, one locus of endurance.

Abysmal images played off into the night.

Made in the USA
Coppell, TX
17 March 2020